Son of
Stupid Men Jokes

Jasmine Birtles

§

Michael O'Mara Books Limited

This edition published in 1994 by
Michael O'Mara Books Limited
9 Lion Yard, Tremadoc Road,
London SW4 7NQ

Copyright © 1994 by Michael O'Mara Books
Limited

A CIP catalogue record for this book is
available from the British Library.

ISBN 1-85479-989-4
Printed and bound by Cox and Wyman,
Reading.

10 9 8 7 6 5 4 3 2

What's the difference between a man and a shopping trolley?

§

A shopping trolley has a mind of its own.

How many men does it take to change a lightbulb?

§

Ten - One to put it in and nine to congratulate him down at the pub.

Stupid man to his doctor: 'Doctor, you've got to help me. Every morning, regular as clockwork, my bowels move at seven o'clock.' Doctor: 'What's wrong with that?' Stupid man: 'I don't get up till nine.'

Why are mother-in-law jokes so simple?

§

So men can find them funny.

Why are Catholic men like British Rail trains?

§

They never pull out in time.

Why doesn't Santa Claus have any children?

§

Because he only comes once a year.

'Am I your first?' asked the Latin lover after sex.

§

'You might be,' she replied, 'you look familiar.'

What goes in dry, comes out warm and wet and gives a lot of satisfaction?

§

A tea-bag.

When is the safest time for sex?

§

When your husband's away.

'Mummy what's an orgasm?'

§

'I dunno love, ask your dad.'

A couple decided to smuggle a skunk into the country. When they got to the Customs desk the creature tried to struggle out of the suitcase. 'Quick,' said the wife to the husband, 'stuff it down your pants.' 'What about the smell?' he said. 'Well, if it dies, it dies,' she replied.

My boyfriend's got a photographic brain - it never developed.

Why do some men claim to be sexual athletes?

§

Because they always come first.

'Do you ever talk to your husband when you're making love?'

§

'Only if he telephones.'

There are three types of men: Tri-weekly, Try weekly, and Try weakly.

Men fantasize about being in bed with two women. Women fantasize about it too because at least they'll have someone to talk to when he falls asleep.

Why do women still like to have a man around?

§

Because vibrators can't mow the lawn.

What's six inches long and gets women excited?

§

A £50 note.

Did you ever hear about the man who said he could have any woman he pleased?

§

Shame he never pleased any.

D'you think my body's dynamite?' asked Mr Wonderful. 'Possibly,' she replied, 'but it's a shame it's got such a short fuse.'

Did you hear about the man who was so stupid he thought an organ grinder was a condom full of sand?

'C'mon darling, don't play hard
to get!'

§

'I'm not, I'm playing impossible to get.'

'Hello darlin', do you come
here often?'

§

'No, and now that I know you're here I
won't come at all.'

'Hey darlin', d'you wanna see the biggest prick in this room?'

§

'No thanks, I think I've already met him.'

Man: How do you like your eggs in the morning?

§

Woman: Unfertilized!

Having undressed for a first night of passion, Mr Wonderful stood admiringly in front of the mirror. 'I had to fight hard for this body, you know,' he said. 'Oh yeah?' she said, bored. 'Shame you lost.'

On a one-night stand the woman praised her lover for being so active. 'Well,' smirked the man, 'that's because I've been in the VD clinic for the last six weeks.' 'Oh yes,' she replied, 'what's the food like? I'm going in tomorrow.'

What's the difference between a great lover and a pervert?

§

A great lover uses a feather; a pervert uses the whole chicken.

What's the difference between the M1 and a boring man?

§

You can turn off the M1.

Why won't a man put a woman on a pedestal once he's married her?

§

Because, on a pedestal, women can't reach to clean the floor.

What's the quickest way for a woman to lose 12 stone of unwanted fat?

§

Divorce him.

Marriage is a good way for a woman to spend her time until the right man comes along.

Beware the man who offers to give you something you've never had before. He's probably got VD.

What's the real reason men can't communicate?

§

It's hard to talk and drink beer at the same time.

What do you give the man who has everything?

§

Penicillin.

How can you tell if a man has animal magnetism?

§

He attracts fleas.

What do you say to a man who doesn't believe in free love?

§

'That'll be fifty quid please.'

Men's first experience of life is trying to get out of a woman's body and then they spend the rest of their lives trying to get back in.

A man I met in a bar said he was a late-starter. His father's stories about the birds and the bees were so interesting he was 38 before he got interested in women.

Husband: 'Why don't you ever tell me when you have an orgasm?'

§

Wife: 'Because you're never there.'

What's the definition of a faithful husband?

§

One whose alimony cheques arrive on time.

My husband's very sensitive about his hair - I don't know why because he hasn't got any.

How do you know when a man has found his intellectual equal?

§

He's just picked up a broom-handle.

What's the difference between a clitoris and a pub?

§

Men can always find a pub.

My husband died at sea. He would
have sent out an SOS but he couldn't
spell it.

§

I met my husband at a dance and he
was the best-looking man on the
floor ... I can see him now, lying there.

This man heard the country was at war - so he moved to the city.

§

My husband added some magic to our marriage - he disappeared.

Why are men like bank accounts?

§

One day they're up, the next they're down, and most of the time they show no interest.

'Do you think my husband's ugly?'

§

'Well not exactly, but he's got the perfect face for radio.'

What usually happens when a man puts his best foot forward?

§

It ends up in his mouth.

What do most women miss when they stop being single?

§

Having sex.

How are men like dogs about housework?

§

They run and hide every time they see the vacuum cleaner.

What do electric trains and breasts have in common?

§

They're both intended for children but it's the fathers that end up playing with them.

My husband is a well-known speaker. He can talk for hours without a note, and for that matter, without a point.

My friend Sue has just chucked her boyfriend because each time they had sex he said 'This is fun ... wasn't it.'

He said, 'What would you say if I asked you to marry me?' I said, 'Nothing, I can't talk and laugh at the same time.'

You know women's problem? They get all excited about nothing - and then marry him!

§

Definition of a boring man: one who, when you ask him how he is, insists on telling you.

My friends said my baby looked just like his father - then they turned him the right way up.

Did you hear about the guy who was so stupid he called in Rentokil because he found a nest of tables in his living room?

Where can you find the best selection of men's socks?

§

On the bedroom floor.

Why do women have a higher threshold of pain?

§

They need it to put up with men.

A stupid man visited our local museum yesterday and there was a sign saying 'Wet Floor' - so he did.

§

Plumber: 'Where's the drip?'
Wife: 'He's in the bathroom trying to fix the leak.'

My boss told me he wanted some old-fashioned loving. So I introduced him to my grandmother.

I had to divorce my husband. He couldn't stand me when I was drunk and I couldn't stand him when I was sober.

What do you call your husband when he turns up with flowers?

§

Guilty.

What do you call a man who opens the car door for you?

§

A chauffeur.

I know this guy who's so stupid when he wants to count to 21 he has to drop his trousers.

§

A man heard that most car accidents take place within two miles of home. So he moved.

My husband is so forgetful that this morning he stood in front of the mirror for half an hour trying to remember where he'd seen himself before.

More husbands would leave home if they knew how to pack.

§

Did you hear about the man who was so stupid he looked both ways before crossing his legs?

What would a smart woman do if she found her husband in bed with another woman? She'd grab the woman's white stick and beat her out of the house with it.

Why don't men show their feelings?

§

What feelings?

What is a man's idea of honesty in a relationship?

§

Telling you his real name.

How is an ex-husband like an inflamed appendix?

§

It gave you a lot of pain and after it was removed, you found you didn't need it anyway.

Where do you have to go to find a committed man?

§

A mental hospital.

My husband's great at parties - he can
brighten up a room just by leaving it.

§

He's not a steady drinker - his hands
shake too much.

Why are men always happy?

§

Because ignorance is bliss.

Why do scientists like to study men's brains?

§

Because they've never been used.

My man started his career as a dishwasher in a greasy spoon café, but he never lived up to his early promise.

Two men were sitting in a bar and one was complaining to the other: 'My girlfriend says I'm a lousy lover, but I don't agree. After all, how can you make a judgment like that in two minutes?'

What do you call a man who tidies up
after himself?

§

An over-achiever.

Did you hear about the guy who was so stupid he thought monogamy was what sideboards were made of?

Why is it no use for a woman to tell a man to get lost?

§

Because most of them already are.

Why do men have an inferiority complex?

§

Because they are.

What's a man's idea of a balanced diet?

§

A hamburger in each hand.

How do you stop a man from drowning?

§

Take your foot off his head.

Why do men complain women have no sense of humour when they have no sense and even less humour?

Did you hear about the guy who thought that manual labour was a Spanish trade union official?

When confronted by two evils, choose the handsomest one.

§

Three wise men? You've got to be joking!

Be kind to animals - hug a man today.

§

Going to bed with some men can lead
to a foetal error.

Did you hear about the stupid man who was so argumentative he wouldn't even eat food that agreed with him?

No one could accuse my husband of being two-faced. If he were he would hardly be wearing the one he's got now.

How many men does it take to change a lightbulb?

§

Who cares, you can never get them to do anything anyway.

Why did the man cross the road?

§

Who knows why they do anything.

Eve was the first feminist: she tried to bring about the fall of man.

§

Men are like Chinese food - they satisfy you, but only for a short time.

My husband's not all bad - he's a very modest man, but then he's got a lot to be modest about.

My husband's so bad at geography he thinks El Salvador is a Mexican bullfighter.

How did the stupid man burn his face?

§

He went bobbing for chips.

What did your boyfriend get on his IQ test?'

§

'Drool.'

My husband came home
from the car-wash
dripping with water -
he'd forgotten to take the car.

'Mummy, mummy, now that I'm 14, can I start wearing a bra?'

§

'Shut up, Henry, you're a boy.'

What's a man's idea of helping around the house?

§

Putting the toilet seat down.

If small is beautiful my husband is
a phallic thimble.

§

My husband is a self-made man and
he worships his creator.

There are only two things my boyfriend can't stand - sexism, and women who insist on being treated as equals.

Did you hear about the stupid man who thought innuendo was an Italian suppository?

What's the difference between men and chimps?

§

One is hairy, smelly and scratches his bum. The other is a chimp.

Sex with a man is all right but it's not as good as the real thing.

§

My husband's so stupid he thinks fellatio is a character in *Hamlet*.

My husband's so stupid he thinks mutual orgasm is an insurance company.

This man snored so loudly he used to wake himself up, so he started sleeping in the next room.

What is a woman's favourite piece of household equipment?

§

A husband with a large bank account.

What's the definition of a perfect man?

§

One with a 12-inch tongue and a wallet to match.

What's the difference between men and bananas?

§

Some women like bananas.

What is a woman's best cure for loneliness?

§

Being single.

Stupid man: 'Hey darlin', girls don't call me "Big Willie" for nothing.'

Woman: 'No, you have to pay them.'

Did you hear about the man who was so stupid he thought coq au vin was sex in a truck?

Man: Doctor, doctor, I haven't been myself lately.

§

Doctor: Sounds like a great improvement.

Why do married women make great comedians?

§

They're used to getting no response.

What's the difference between a man and a book of sexual etiquette?

§

About 20,000 words.

'My boyfriend's got Hermes.'

'Surely you mean Herpes?'

'No, he's the carrier.'

Wife: 'Shall I cut your sandwich into two or four pieces?'

§

Husband: 'Better make it two -
I couldn't manage four.'

Did you hear about the stupid man who tried to get high on coke?

§

The bubbles kept going up his nose.

My husband's mind is like a Welsh
railway - one track and dirty.

§

Don't go to bed angry -
stay up and fight.

'How long can a man live without a brain?'

§

'That depends - how old's your husband?'

I know this guy who loves bargains so much he'll buy anything that's marked down. Last week he came home with an escalator.

Men don't get excited about women's minds, they get excited about what they don't mind.

How do men define an equal relationship?

§

You cook, they eat; you tidy, they mess up; you nurse, they're taken care of.

What's the definition of a tragedy?

§

Marrying a man for love and then discovering that he has no money.

What's the difference between a puppy and a new husband?

§

After two years, the dog is still pleased to see you.

Why do women cry at weddings?

§

You'd cry too if you knew the men they're marrying.

I knew a man once whose ambition was to be the last man on earth so that he could find out if all those women were telling him the truth.

'What have you got in common
with your husband?'
§
'We were both married on
the same day.'

Better to have loved and lost than to have spent your whole damn life with him.

§

Marriage is a fine institution, but who wants to live in an institution?

'I can talk to my husband about any subject I like ... he won't understand it, but I can talk to him.'

What does it mean to come home to a man who'll give you some love and tenderness?

§

You're in the wrong house.

What's the kindest thing you can say about men?

§

They're bio-degradable.

Woman: 'Do you file your nails?'

§

Man: 'No, I cut them off and throw
them away.'

Why do men act like idiots?

§

Who says they're acting?

Why can't men make ice-cubes?

§

They can't find the recipe.

**What do you call an intelligent,
sensitive man?**

§

Extinct.

Not all women are silly - some are single.

§

Beware the man who says he'll drive you wild - he's got rabies.

Man: 'Doctor, doctor, what's wrong with me?'
Doctor: 'You're mad.'

Man: 'Ha! I want a second opinion.'

Doctor: 'All right, you're stupid as well.'

What word best describes most of the men in singles bars?

§

Married.

What's the difference between a man and a chocolate bar?

§

A chocolate bar will satisfy a woman every time.

Working for a man is like smoking dope - the harder you suck, the higher you get.

What's the difference between a man and a gorilla?

§

A gorilla doesn't leave so much hair in the bath.

How do you find out what life is like without a man around?

§

Get married.

What is a man's idea of a seven-course meal?

§

A burger and a six-pack.

What's the difference between a husband and a lover?

§

About four hours.

How many men does it take to dirty the whole kitchen when cooking a meal?

§

One.

Women don't smoke after sex because one drag a night is enough.

How are men like microwave meals?

§

30 seconds and they're done.

How are men like toothpaste tubes?

§

One squeeze and they're all over you.

How do you get something hard and throbbing between your legs?

§

Buy a motorbike.

'**Do you believe in sex before marriage?**'

§

'Not if it delays the ceremony.'

My husband's at home recovering from a freak accident - he was suddenly struck by a thought.

What's the difference between an intelligent man and a stupid man?

§

Nothing, they both think they know everything.

How many men does it take to change a roll of loo paper?

§

Don't know - it's never happened.

What's the smallest book in the world?

§

'What Men Know About Women.'

How can you tell if a man's been in the kitchen?

§

The fire brigade is coming out.

What's yellow and would look good on any man?

§

A JCB.

What's the best way to a man's heart?

§

Who cares?

After 20 years of marriage I'm finally developing an attachment for my husband - it fits over his mouth.

He makes love like he drives his car - he goes too fast and gets there before anyone else.

What's the difference between a man and a tomato?

§

A tomato isn't a real vegetable.

How can you tell if a man is lying?

§

His lips are moving.

Did you hear about the dyslexic bloke who went to a toga party dressed as a goat?

§

Never touch a man who says he'll grow on you - he'll give you warts.

Impersonate a man -
have a lobotomy.

§

Don't wake up grumpy -
let him lie in.

My husband and I divorced on the grounds of irreconcilable differences: he's a man and I'm a woman.